KAPPIANAQTUT

KAPPIANAQTUT

Strange Creatures and Fantastic Beings from Inuit Myths and Legends

Volume 1:

The Mother of the Sea Beasts & The Giants of the North

Researched and Written by

Neil Christopher

Illustrated by

Mike Austin

Published in Canada by Inhabit Media Inc. (www.inhabitmedia.com)

Printed and bound in Canada.

ISBN 978-1-926569-38-3

Project Editors: Neil Christopher and Louise Flaherty
Researcher and Writer: Neil Christopher
Illustrator: Mike Austin
Translators: Louise Flaherty and Robert Joanas

Library and Archives Canada Cataloguing in Publication

Kappianaqtut : strange creatures and fantastic beings from Inuit myths and legends / researched and written by Neil Christopher ; illustrated by Mike Austin. -- 2nd ed.

Includes bibliographical references.
Contents: v. 1. The mother of the sea beasts & the giants of the North.
ISBN 978-1-926569-38-3

1. Inuit mythology. 2. Inuit--Folklore. 1. Inuit--Folklore.
I. Christopher, Neil, 1972- II. Austin, Mike

E99.E7C5464 2011 398.2089'9712 C2011-902077-7

This is the first in the *Kappianaqtut: Strange Creatures and Fantastic Beings from Inuit Myths and Legends* series. There are hundreds of supernatural beings in Inuit myths and legends and, as such, the series has been divided into separate volumes. Each volume has a specific focus and is designed to stand on its own. The series introduction has been included with each volume to ensure the reader has some background in the storytelling traditions of the Inuit.

Volume I explores the giants of the North and the mother of the sea mammals. These beings were chosen for the first book in the series because they are common characters in Inuit myths and legends and can be readily found in the storytelling traditions of almost all Inuit groups.

Contents

Editor's Note

Whenever possible the original stories and Inuktitut orthography are used in this text without modification. Occassionally, when the original Inuktitut orthography is confusing, the term has been rewritten using the current standardized Inuktitut writing system. Several words throughout the text were not recognizable by the translator, and it was decided that these words should be left in their original form.

Inuit stories vary from region to region. Many stories are similar, with slight variations. Whenever it is unclear if stories and characters are unique or simply variations of each other, I have erred on the side of diversity by including all of them.

Acknowledgements

I seem to have a lot of great ideas but, unfortunately, I am not a talented writer. So, to start, I must thank Noel McDermott, Anna Ziegler, Keith Christopher, and Donna Christopher for their help and patience. This manuscript would never have been completed without their tireless assistance. I am grateful to the following people who have provided me with guidance, assistance, and support throughout this project: Louise Flaherty, Susan Sammons, Joe Karetak, Nellie Kusugak, Rebecca Hainnu, Pujjuut Kusugak, Maaki Kakkik, Eva Noah, Saa Pitseolak, Ooloota Maatiusi, Uvinik Qamaniq, Leah Otak, and John MacDonald.

A special note of gratitude needs to go to Mike Austin, my good friend and the illustrator of this project. Without his excitement and creative vision, this project would have never been realized.

This book is primarily a collection of quotations, passages, and knowledge collected from Inuit informants over the last century. Over the past ten years I have collected and read anything I could find on the traditional stories of the Inuit. During that time I have had the opportunity to listen to, and discuss, various topics of Inuit mythology and history with many knowledgeable Nunavummiut. I have collected and organized the information I uncovered and have presented much of it unaltered in this text. I am sincerely grateful to the ethnographers and Inuit informants for recording and sharing this information so that it would be available to future generations.

Here are some of the people whose research and knowledge contributed to this book.

Arranged in alphabetical order according to first name.

Atqáralâq
Aua
Babah Kalluk
Celina Kalluk
Edward William Nelson
E. W. Hawkes
Franz Boas
George Kappianaq
Henry Isluanik
Knud Rasmussen
Laakuluk Williamson
Louise Flaherty
Lucien M. Turner
Marianne Pujuat Taparti
Mark Kalluak
Nâlungiaq
Naomie Idlout
Oingoot Kalluk
Peter Atsiqtaq
Rhoda Karetak
Simon Idlout
Zipporah Kalluk

Foreword
for the Second Edition

A great deal has been set down concerning Inuit mythological beings, with the interesting result that many accounts of such entities seem to conflict or vary wildly. Reasons for the discordance often boil down to a general ignorance or disinterest, on the part of those who are rendering such accounts, in conveying the rich psychological and spiritual "language" of traditional Inuit. Inuit are known for speaking obliquely. The ability to use implication, rather than assertive statements, is often a cultural mark of wisdom. Much of this implicative convention stems from the respect for *isuma* ("personal identity/inclinations") that traditionally held a sacred place in Inuit culture. This manifested as a love of allusive knowledge, in the belief that only an individual who has sought out and actively plucked a lesson from interaction with others is one who has truly learned. The other side of this convention was the fact of a teacher's own isuma. The teacher had the right to withdraw knowledge if faced with a student who evinced disinclination to be wisely *uimanngittuq* ("not in a hurry"; i.e., not easily frazzled). We might then say that Inuit wisdom, especially as it appears in stories, is "encoded." Phraseology, terminology, in-story songs, turns of event—these are laced with double or triple meanings, spiritual or ethical subtext, and ontological exploration. Tragically, many of the oldest written sources of Inuit material

(Rasmussen being a notable exception) have diminished the stories via syncretic interpretation or a misapplied desire for brevity.

Nevertheless, the superior oral forms have defied expectations, surviving among Inuit into the present era, with proof of the tradition's integrity lying in the fact that story motifs, even terminological delineations, evince astonishing concordance around the circumpolar world. Recent works have, therefore, been able to take a restorative approach, so to speak, in the presentation of Inuit cosmology, by comparing the most respectable colonial accounts with often-unprecedented recordings of elders speaking in the old conventions and archaisms by which the Inuit world once turned. *Kappianaqtut* is one of these recent works, remarkable for its blend of academic tidiness with an understanding of the Inuit worldview. This volume's primary concerns, Nuliajuk and the giants, are pivotal facets of Inuit cosmogony—superficially monstrous, sensationalistic, but linked via traditional subtext to high Inuit philosophy.

The tales discuss concepts such as *uumaniq* (in literal Inuktitut, "rawest life-force"; philosophically, the urge of instinct/ passion itself), *innua* ("humanness"; philosophically, awareness), and *anirniq* (literally, "breath"; philosophically, interface with the numinous). But our advice, as in facing any Inuit story, is to avoid seeking assertive statements when encountering the text for the first time. As in hearing the roundabout advice of an elder, it is worth being uimanngittuq, letting the tales wash, like formless tides, over all layers of one's mind. Subtextual awareness may arise hours, days, even years later. For an Inuit story is never independent. It is always but a strand in a vast web of knowledge. One might even argue that there is no such thing as a single Inuit tale, for each telling is a bundle, like a riddle with no set answer. How can this sort of lore demand anything other than patience in both reception and presentation? The latter, *Kappianaqtut* accomplishes eminently well.

Rachel A. Qitsualik and Sean A. Tinsley

Original Foreword
(from the First Edition)

I have always felt a pull to the North. Perhaps the stories I read from Farley Mowat and Jack London influenced me more than I care to admit. But one day during my year at teachers' college, I walked by a small job notice, roughly cut from a newspaper and tacked up onto a bulletin board, that was advertising teaching positions in the Arctic. I quickly responded to the ad and a few months later, in August of 1997, I found myself standing wide-eyed on the shore of Resolute Bay without a clue in the world of what I was getting myself into.

That first year in the High Arctic was one of the most influential of my life. For the first time, I experienced a place where the weather still had power over the activities of the day. I met people with a history and a view of life that was a world apart from my own. In this cold and dark place, for the first time in my life, I experienced the warmth and comfort of being a part of a small community.

During the three years I taught in Resolute, I was introduced to traditional Inuit stories. My students shared with me legends of strange creatures that lived in this windswept world. It was there that my interest in Inuit mythology began. It is the people of Resolute Bay—who shared with me their time and knowledge, and allowed me to feel part of their community—who started me on this quest to understand the North and the unusual creatures that are said to inhabit this unique place.

I must confess that it wasn't only the people I met that started me on my journey, it was also the place. The land, the sky, and the sea made me believe that there could be things in this world that remain unseen to most of us. The longer I lived in the North and experienced the cold, the darkness, the huge sky, the constantly drifting snow, and the blizzards, the more I could believe that this place was controlled by other forces. I clearly remember a particularly bad blizzard during my first dark season in Resolute. I was excited to experience a winter storm. I bundled myself up with warm clothing and headed outside to feel the storm's power. As soon as I stepped from the protection of my doorway, I was batted around by the storm. I felt exhilarated by the strong wind and blinding snow. Until, slowly, I began to sense I was being watched. Squinting against the whipping wind, I looked out into the blizzard to see if I could distinguish anything behind the sheets of snow. But the snow blowing into my eyes prevented me from seeing clearly. I tried to shake off the sensation; however, the feeling stayed with me. It felt as if there was something waiting for me to move a little farther from town, away from safety. I quickly went back into my house and spent the better part of the evening staring out of the window into the storm. I sometimes think back to that day and wonder if there was something in the blizzard, patiently waiting for me to make a mistake.

When I left Resolute to go back to university, I began looking for a book that would provide me with more information on the fantastic Arctic beings I had heard about. I searched for some time, but I never found the book I was looking for. I found that many explorers and researchers had gathered stories from different regions but most of these books were out of print or hard to find. When I arrived back in the North two years later, I searched through old books in my spare time and talked with elders to get more information on these stories and beings. Finally I decided that it was my turn to put together a book for people like me, who love to read about mythological beings and imagine a world still filled with magic and unknown mysteries.

So, quite simply, this is the book I looked for but never found. I hope you like it.

Neil Christopher
Iqaluit, Nunavut, 2007

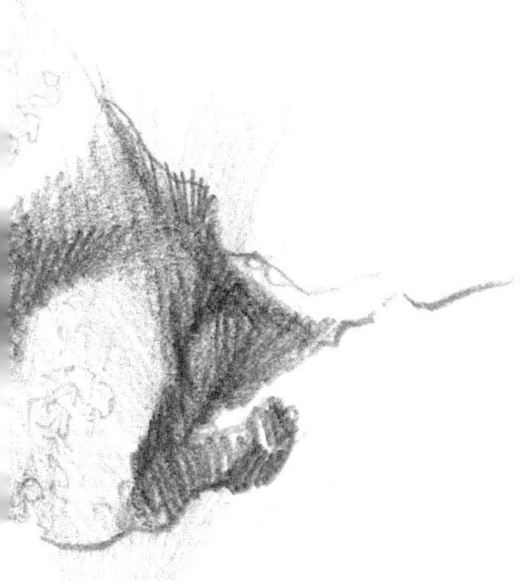

KAPPIANAQTUT

Introduction

> But what you have asked me about, and what I am going to tell you about, is something that is known to every child, every child that has been hushed to sleep with a story by its mother. Children are full of life, they never want to sleep. Only a song or monotonous words can make them quieten down so that at last they fall asleep. That is why mothers and grandmothers always put little children to sleep with tales. It is from them we all have our knowledge, for children never forget. (Nâlungiaq, in Rasmussen, 1931, p. 207)

Inuit myths and legends come from another time, from an age long since past, when the world was still young and all things were possible. During this magical time, animals and humans could communicate and even intermarry. It was a time when humans could transform into animals and animals could transform into humans, and often did. In those ancient days, words were magic and thoughts could send people across massive distances within seconds.

In those early times, giants lived in the North and warred with each other. It was a time when evil deeds and disrespectful behavior transformed the souls of animals and humans into vengeful spirits. These specters populated the sky, the land, and the sea.

It is sometimes hard to understand the stories from that magical time. When you read Inuit myths and legends, remember that these old stories do not follow the rules of the present, because in ancient times these rules did not yet exist. In 1923, Nâlungiaq, a Netsilingmiut informant, explained to Knud Rasmussen what the world was like in the beginning:

> In the very first times there was no light on earth. Everything was in darkness, the lands could not be seen, the animals could not be seen. And still, both people and animals lived on the earth, but there was no difference between them. They lived promiscuously: a person could become an animal, and an animal could become a human being. There were wolves, bears, and foxes but as soon as they turned into humans they were all the same. They may have had different habits, but all spoke the same tongue, lived in the same kind of house, and spoke and hunted in the same way.
>
> That is the way they lived here on earth in the very earliest times, times that no one can understand now. That was the time when magic words were made. A word spoken by chance would suddenly become powerful, and what people wanted to happen could happen, and nobody could explain how it was. (Rasmussen, 1931, p. 208)

Between 1921 and 1923, Knud Rasmussen spent a great deal of time travelling across the north, interviewing Inuit about their beliefs and customs. He realized that the stories the Inuit informants shared with him were more than just stories. These narratives come from somewhere in between myth and history, fact and fantasy, as can be seen in the following quotation:

> …Nâlungiaq had an excellent opportunity to show how in many respects their religion is entirely based

> upon the tales. For all that is described in them did really happen once, when everything in the world was different to what it is now. Thus these tales are both their real history and the source of all their religious ideas. (Rasmussen, 1931, p. 207)

To put these stories and beliefs into perspective, it is important to imagine what life was like for Inuit. Most Inuit groups lived without access to wood or metal. Many relied on migratory animals for clothing and food. And all of them had to survive in a harsh and dangerous climate.

When Rasmussen travelled to the Iglulik region and interviewed Inuit, he met Aua. Aua was a great *angakkuq* (shaman) and was perhaps one of the most insightful and articulate Inuit informants ever recorded. Aua and the group of Inuit that he lived with held many shared beliefs and customs. For these Inuit, their daily activities were influenced by various taboos and rules that needed to be followed. Many times Rasmussen asked the Inuit informants to explain the reasons behind their taboos and the rules of life the community followed. All the members of the camp could recite the rules they lived by, but none of them offered any reason or justification for these prescriptions on how to live.

In *Intellectual Culture of the Iglulik Eskimo*, Rasmussen recorded a poignant exchange between Aua and himself. According to Rasmussen's notes, Aua, like all the other members of the community, did not know how to respond to the constant questioning about taboos. One day, Aua decided to turn the question "why?" back to the ethnographer. Aua began:

> In order to hunt well and live happily, man must have calm weather. Why this constant succession of blizzards and all this needless hardship for men seeking food for themselves and those they care for? Why? Why? (Rasmussen, 1929, p. 55)

To these questions, Rasmussen had no answer. Aua led Rasmussen into a neighbouring iglu and continued:

> Why should it be cold and comfortless in here? Kublo has been out hunting all day, and if he had got a seal, as he deserved, his wife would now be sitting laughing beside her lamp, letting it burn full, without fear of having no blubber left for tomorrow. The place would be warm and bright and cheerful. The children would come out from under their rugs and enjoy life. Why should it not be so? Why? (Rasmussen, 1929, p. 55)

Once again, Rasmussen was without answer. Finally, Aua brought him into the iglu of his sister who was very ill. Aua spoke once again:

> Why must people be ill and suffer pain? We are all afraid of illness. Here is this old sister of mine; as far as anyone can see, she has done no evil; she has lived through a long life and given birth to healthy children, and now she must suffer before her days end. Why? Why? (Rasmussen, 1929, p. 55)

Rasmussen was silent. How could anyone answer these questions? What Aua said next is the most concise and illuminating passage I have ever read on the origin of Inuit mythology. Aua, the great angakkuq, said:

> You are equally unable to give any reason when we ask you why life is as it is. And so it must be. All our customs come from life and turn towards life; we explain nothing, we believe nothing, but in what I have just shown you lies our answer to all you ask.
>
> We fear the weather spirit of earth, that we must fight against to wrest our food from land and sea. We fear Sila.

> We fear dearth and hunger in the cold snow huts.
>
> We fear Takanakapsaluk, the great woman down at the bottom of the sea, that rules over all the beasts of the sea.
>
> We fear the sickness that we meet with daily all around us; not death, but the suffering. We fear the evil spirits of life, those of the air, of the sea and the earth, that can help wicked shamans to harm their fellow men.
>
> We fear the souls of dead human beings and of the animals we have killed.
>
> Therefore it is that our fathers have inherited from their fathers all the old rules of life which are based on the experience and wisdom of generations. We do not know how, we cannot say why, but we keep those rules in order that we may live untroubled. And so ignorant are we in spite of all our shamans, that we fear everything unfamiliar. We fear what we see about us, and we fear all the invisible things that are likewise about us, all that we have heard of in our forefathers' stories and myths. Therefore we have our customs, which are not the same as those of the white men, the white men who live in another land and have need of other ways. (Rasmussen, 1929, p. 55-56)

Aua's explanation silenced Rasmussen. Aua's younger brother, Ivaluardjuk, took advantage of the break in conversation to offer some additional information. Ivaluardjuk's words lend additional insight into the world in which these myths and legends originate. As can be seen from Ivaluardjuk's quotation, these Inuit lived in a land of consequence:

> The greatest peril of life lies in the fact that human food consists entirely of souls.

> All the creatures that we have to kill and eat, all those that we have to strike down and destroy to make clothes for ourselves, have souls, like we have, souls that do not perish with the body, and which must therefore be propitiated lest they should revenge themselves on us for taking away their bodies. (Rasmussen, 1929, p. 56)

Nâlungiaq, Aua, and Ivaluardujuk's gifted explanations of ancient times, hardships and Inuit beliefs provide a valuable context for these traditional stories. When reading the subsequent chapters of this book, it will be valuable to keep their words close.

There is one last point about Inuit mythology that should be mentioned. Many of the beings described in this book are not simply the result of imaginative storytellers. I spoke to people who have had personal experiences with the fantastic creatures presented in this publication. Often these creatures were not sighted by a lone hunter, but rather, by a group of people out on the land. Several elders I interviewed confirmed that many of these beings did exist at one time and they assured me that, although scarce, some of these beings still live in remote regions.

The Mother of the Sea Mammals

The mother of the sea mammals is arguably the most important mythological being for many Inuit groups. It is at her whim that Inuit starve or live comfortably. Stories depict her as a proud woman who refused to accept a husband. In many versions of the story, she was deceived and mistreated by the spirit of a fulmar. And in the end, her father sacrificed her to save himself. Her short life made her bitter and angry and her death brought her power over the lives of Inuit. She is the mother of the sea beasts, and some stories give her powers over all wildlife in the North. Some Inuit groups attribute even more power to her, believing she can control storms, fog, ice, and wind, and even bring sickness and death directly to Inuit.

The mother of the sea mammals is known by many names. Each region has its own way of referring to her. The following is a list of the names that I have encountered in my search for the young woman who later became the powerful mother of the sea mammals:

Nuliajuk (Netsilik and Iglulik Inuit)
Nulijajuk (Mackenzie Inuit)
Aiviliajuk or *Avilayoq* (Iglulik Inuit)
Arnakapshaluk (Copper Inuit)
Uinigumissuitung or *Uinigumasuittuq* (Baffin Island Inuit)

It seems that after the mortal woman was cast out and became the powerful woman of the sea, she was reborn and, as such, she is referred to by a different set of names. Because Inuit names are generally descriptive, perhaps once this woman became such a mighty and feared being she required new names to describe her. The following is a list of expressions used to refer to her once she has become the mother of the sea mammals:

Sedna or *Sänvna*, “the one down there”
(Cumberland Sound and Davis Strait)

Imam-shua, “the spirit of the sea”
(Chugach)

Nulirahak, “the big woman”
(Asiatic)

Takanakapsaluk or *Takannaaluk*, “the bad one” or “the terrible one down there”
(Iglulik)

Arnaluk takanaluk, “the woman down there”
(Iglulik)

Kavna, “the one down there”
(Netsilik)

Kana, “the one down there”
(Greenland)

Qavna, “the one down there”
(Iglulik)

Kunna or *Katuma,* “the one down there”
(Ponds Bay, Baffin Island)

Arnakusagak or *Arnarquaqssaq*, "the old woman"
(W. Greenland)

Nerrivik, "the food dish" or "the place of food"
(N. Greenland)

Nerrivigssuaq, "the great meat dish"
(N. Greenland)

Nivikaa, "the woman thrown backwards over the edge"
(S. Greenland)

Sättuma eeva, "spirit of the sea depth"
(E. Greenland)

Säsvsuma inua, "spirit of the sea depth"
(W. Greenland)

Sassuna Arnaa, "the mother beneath"
(Greenland)

Nulirah, "old woman"
(Siberia)

Knud Rasmussen, during his ethnographic study of the Inuit, encountered many stories and shamanistic practices that centered around pleasing this woman. The following excerpt from *Intellectual Culture of the Iglulik Eskimo,* published in 1929, helps to illustrate her importance in the lives of the coastal Inuit:

> From her comes all the most indispensable of human food, the flesh of the sea beasts; from her comes the blubber that warms the cold snow huts and gives light in the lamps when the long arctic night broods over the land. From her come also the skins of the great seal which are likewise indispensable for clothes and boot soles, if the hunters are to be able to move over the frozen sea all seasons of the year. But while Takánakapsâluk ("the bad

> one") gives mankind all these good things, created out of her own finger-joints, it is she also who sends nearly all the misfortunes which are regarded by the dwellers on earth as the worst and direst. In her anger at men's failing to live as they should, she calls up storms that prevent the men from hunting, or she keeps the animals they seek hidden away in a pool she has at the bottom of the sea, or she will steal away the souls of human beings and send sickness among the people. It is not strange therefore, that it is regarded as one of a shaman's greatest feats to visit her where she lives at the bottom of the sea, and so tame and conciliate her that human beings can live once more untroubled on earth. (Rasmussen, 1929, p. 123-124)

When considering the stories of this powerful figure, it seems that this woman was not a loved deity, but rather a feared and moody tyrant. Many sources validated this assumption. Another illuminating account recorded by Rasmussen helps illustrate this point:

> [T]he coast dwellers had described their Nuliajuk as a big woman, who had once been seen on the ice and had caused great terror; despite the reverence in which they held "the mother of the animals of the sea," they had attacked her, and she had been harpooned by a certain Qalaseq, a former Netsilik, who now lived at Chesterfield Inlet. She had quickly escaped, however. (Rasumussen, 1930, p. 49)

It is usually accepted that this woman's home is located at the bottom of the sea. However, in Franz Boas's *Second Report on the Eskimo of Baffin Land and Hudson Bay* I found a reference to other locations where you might find this powerful being:

> All dangerous places, like tide-rifts and stormy capes, are believed to be the favorite haunts of Nuliayoq. For this reason, all taboos must be observed there with particular care. (Boas, 1907, p. 498)

Although command over animals, weather, and illness is attributed to this woman of the sea, the means of her control can be difficult to comprehend. The following explanation recorded by Rasmussen helps clarify this being's means of control:

> She rules through tuurngait [spirits], both the ordinary tuurngait and tuurngait kiglerigtut [evil spirits]. By means of these she either makes the animals visible and easy to hunt, so that people have food enough and clothing and warmth, or she makes them invisible, lets them disappear entirely, so that mankind has to go hungry and cold.
>
> Through the same spirits she can influence wind and weather, especially blizzards, which prevents hunting trips and hunting at the breathing holes. (Rasmussen, 1931, p. 224)

It is through her control of spirits, both evil and benign, that she is able to influence all aspects of life. In this way, perhaps, it is appropriate to view the mother of the sea as a kind of powerful *angakkuq* (shaman) whose influence is dependant on her control of *tuurngait* (helping spirits).

When the mother of the sea mammals becomes angry at the disrespectful behavior of Inuit, she commands her tuurngait to hide or gather the animals, to send bad weather so hunting becomes difficult, and even to bring sickness directly to the Inuit who offend her. Only a powerful angakkuq can approach and appease her. In Hinrich Rink's collection of Inuit stories, there is brief reference to the sea mother from Greenland. Here we have a glimpse at an encounter between an angakkuq and this powerful woman:

> An angakok performed a conjuration in order to procure good seal-hunting. He went down to the old hag, the

> arnarkuagsak, at the bottom of the sea, and found her in a great rage. Having entered her abode, she seized hold of her hair behind one ear, grasping some bloody clothes, and afterwards from behind the other one she fetched down a crying baby, flinging both upon the floor. The angakok then succeeded in propitiating her. (Rink, 1875, p. 466)

The mother of the sea mammals can be angered by the actions of an individual. Often her displeasure is felt by the entire group, but occasionally, she exacts revenge on the offending individual or family. This next story was shared by a Netsilngmiut. It demonstrates the potential consequences of not respecting the rules imposed by the mother of the sea:

> There was once a family that had moved out on to the sea ice to hunt seal. It was early in the winter, and they had just come from those parts of the country inland where they had been hunting caribou since the beginning of autumn. When a family comes down from the interior, they are strictly forbidden to sew new caribou skins on the ice, for all sewing must be done with while they are still on land, in the first snow huts of the autumn. But these people who had now moved out on to the ice failed to observe this important rule, and the wife set about sewing a dress of young caribou calf skins for her son. On the same day, a hurricane burst on them, the ice broke up just behind their snow hut, though it remained firm farther in, where other seal hunters had built their huts; and through the first cracks made by the storm in the ice could be seen a young caribou calf and a marmot swimming about among the breaking pieces. Thus the Sea Spirit made it clear to men that the land animals had been offended by the action of men out on the sea ice. This was her way of showing it, by letting a caribou calf and a little marmot swim about in the rough sea. All the people from the huts near by saw them, and then they disappeared as mysteriously as they had come; but the moment they vanished, the snow hut in

> which the offence had been committed fell into the sea and was swallowed up, with all who dwelt therein. They were drowned, and their souls went down to Takánakapsfîluk, who thus took vengeance upon those that scornfully disregarded the ancient rules of life laid down by their forefathers. (Rasmussen, 1931, p. 71)

There are more versions of the sea goddess legend than there are names for her. But one commonality exists in many versions: she was mistreated and sacrificed for selfish reasons. In this chapter, several versions of her story are included.

The first version presented in this collection was recorded by Franz Boas and published in 1888. Boas recorded this account from Inuit in the Cumberland Sound and Davis Strait area. In this story, Sedna is the name used to refer to the mother of the sea mammals:

> Once upon a time there lived on a solitary shore an Inung with his daughter Sedna. His wife had been dead for some time and the two led a quiet life. Sedna grew up to be a handsome girl and the youths came from all around to sue for her hand, but none of them could touch her proud heart. Finally, at the breaking up of the ice in the spring a fulmar flew from over the ice and wooed Sedna with enticing song. "Come to me," it said; "come into the land of the birds, where there is never hunger, where my tent is made of the most beautiful skins. You shall rest on soft bearskins. My fellows, the fulmars, shall bring you all your heart may desire; their feathers shall clothe you; your lamp shall always be filled with oil, your pot with meat." Sedna could not long resist such wooing and they went together over the vast sea. When at last they reached the country of the fulmar, after a long and hard journey, Sedna discovered that her spouse had shamefully deceived her. Her new home was not built of beautiful pelts, but was covered with wretched fishskins, full of holes, that gave free entrance to wind and snow. Instead of soft reindeer skins her bed was

made of hard walrus hides and she had to live on miserable fish, which the birds brought her. Too soon she discovered that she had thrown away her opportunities when in her foolish pride she had rejected the Inuit youth. In her woe she sang: "Aja. O father, if you knew how wretched I am you would come to me and we would hurry away in your boat over the waters. The birds look unkindly upon me the stranger; cold winds roar about my bed; they give me but miserable food. O come and take me back home. Aja."

When a year had passed and the sea was again stirred by warmer winds, the father left his country to visit Sedna. His daughter greeted him joyfully and besought him to take her back home. The father hearing of the outrages wrought upon his daughter determined upon revenge. He killed the fulmar, took Sedna into his boat, and they quickly left the country which had brought so much sorrow to Sedna. When the other fulmars came home and found their companion dead and his wife gone, they all flew away in search of the fugitives. They were very sad over the death of their poor murdered comrade and continue to mourn and cry until this day.

Having flown a short distance they discerned the boat and stirred up a heavy storm. The sea rose in immense waves that threatened the pair with destruction. In this mortal peril the father determined to offer Sedna to the birds and flung her overboard. She clung to the edge of the boat with a death grip. The cruel father then took a knife and cut off the first joints of her fingers. Falling into the sea they were transformed into whales, the nails turning into whalebone. Sedna holding on to the boat more tightly, the second finger joints fell under the sharp knife and swam away as seals (Pagomys foetidus); when the father cut off the stumps of the fingers they became ground seals (Phoca barbata). Meantime the storm subsided, for the fulmars thought Sedna was drowned. The father then allowed her to come into the boat again. But from that time she cherished a deadly hatred against him and swore bitter revenge. After

> they got ashore, she called her dogs and let them gnaw off the feet and hands of her father while he was asleep. Upon this he cursed himself, his daughter, and the dogs which had maimed him; where upon the earth opened and swallowed the hut, the father, the daughter, and the dogs. They have since lived in the land of Adlivun, of which Sedna is the mistress. (Boas, 1888, p. 175-177)

Even within a region, or Inuit group, several versions of the same story can be found. In 1901, Boas published another variation of the sea goddess legend from the Cumberland Sound region. In this version, Avilayoq is the name given to the mortal woman who would become the sea spirit. She is not referred to as Sedna until she acquires her power. Before she becomes the mother of the sea mammals, Avilayoq is said to have mated with a husky and spawned many groups of beings, including Inuit, Europeans, First Nations people, and even some mythic races. Usually, the myth of the sea goddess and the legend of the woman who partnered with a dog are separate stories; however, sometimes they are combined, as in the following example. Like most stories of Nuliajuk, this story starts with a woman who refuses to have a husband:

> In Padli lived a girl named Avilayoq. Since she did not want to have a husband, she was also called Uinigumissuitung. There was a stone in the village, speckled white and red, which transformed itself into a dog and married this girl. She had many children, some of whom were Eskimo, others white men, others Inuarudligat, Ijiqat, and Adlet. The children made a great deal of noise, which annoyed Avilayoq's father, so that he finally took them across to the island Mituaqdjuausiq. Every day Avilayoq sent her husband across to her father's hut to get meat for herself and her children. She hung around his neck a pair of boots that were fastened to a string. The old man filled the boots

with meat, and the dog took them back to the island. One day, while the dog was gone for meat, a man came to the island in his kayak, and called Uiniguniissuitung. "Take your bag and come with me!" he shouted. He had the appearance of a tall, good-looking man, and the woman was well pleased with him. She took her bag, went down to the kayak, and the man paddled away with her. After they had gone some distance, they came to a cake of floating ice. The man stepped out of the kayak on to the ice. Then she noticed that he was quite a small man, and that he appeared large only because he had been sitting on a high seat. Then she began to cry, while he laughed and said, "Oh, you have seen my seat, have you?" Then he went back into his kayak, and they proceeded on their journey.

Finally they came to a place where there were many people and many huts. He pointed out to her a certain hut made of the skins of yearling seals, and told her that it was his, and that she was to go there. They landed. The woman went up to the hut, while he attended to his kayak. Soon he joined her in the hut, and staid [stayed] with her for three or four days before going out again sealing. Her new husband was a petrel.

Meanwhile her father had left the dog, her former husband, at his house, and had gone to look for her on the island. When he did not find her, he returned home, and told the dog to wait for him, as he was going in search of his daughter. He set out in a large boat, travelled about for a long time, and visited many a place before he succeeded in finding her. Finally he came to the place where she lived. He saw many huts, and, without leaving his boat, he shouted and called to his daughter to return home with him. She came down from her hut, and went aboard her father's boat, where he hid her among some skins.

They had not been gone long, when they saw a man in a kayak following them. It was her new husband. Soon he overtook them; and when he came alongside, he asked the young woman to show her hand, as he was very anxious to see at least part of her body; but she did not move. Then he asked her to show her mitten, but she did not respond to his request. In vain he tried in many ways to induce her to show herself; she kept in hiding. Then he began to cry, resting his head on his arms, that were crossed in front of the man-hole of the kayak. Avilayoq's father paddled on as fast as he could, and the man fell far behind.

It was calm at that time, and they continued on their way home. After some time they saw something coming from behind toward their boat. They could not clearly discern it. Sometimes it looked like a man in a kayak. Sometimes

it looked like a petrel. It flew up and down, then skimmed over the water, and finally came up to their boat and went round and round it several times, and then disappeared again. Suddenly ripples appeared, the waters began to rise, and after a short time a gale was raging. The boat was quite a distance from shore. The old man became afraid lest they might be drowned; and, fearing the revenge of his daughter's husband, he threw her into the water. She held on to the gunwale; then the father took his hatchet and chopped off the first joints of her fingers. When they fell into the water, they were transformed into whales, the nails becoming the whalebone. Still she clung to the boat; again he took his hatchet and chopped off the second joints of her fingers. They became transformed into ground-seals. Still she clung to the boat; then he chopped off the last joints of her fingers, which became transformed into seals. Now she clung to the boat with the stumps of her hands, and her father took his steering-oar and knocked out her left eye. She fell backward into the water, and he paddled ashore.

Then he filled with stones the boots in which the dog was accustomed to carry meat to his family, and only covered the top with meat. The dog started to swim across, but when he was halfway the heavy stones dragged him down. He began to sink, and was drowned. A great noise was heard while he was drowning. The father took down his tent and went down to the beach at the time of low water. There he lay down, and covered himself with the tent. The flood tide rose over him, and when the waters receded he had disappeared.

The woman became Sedna, who lives in the lower world, in her house built of stone and whale-ribs. She has but one eye, and she cannot walk, but slides along, one leg bent under, the other stretched out. Her father lives with her in her house, and lies there covered up with his tent. The dog lives at the door of her house. (Boas, 1901, p. 163-165)

The Netsilik Inuit have a slightly different version of the sea goddess legend. In this story, told by a Netsilingmiut named Nâlungiaq, the mortal woman who becomes the mother of the sea mammals is depicted as a mistreated orphan. In this region, she is known as Nuliajuk.

> Once in times long past people left the settlement at Qingniertôq in Sherman Inlet. They were going to cross the water and had made rafts of kayaks tied together. They were many and were in haste to get away to new hunting grounds. And there was not much room on the rafts they tied together.
>
> At the village there was a little girl whose name was Nuliajuk. She jumped out on to the raft together with the other boys and girls, but no one cared about her, no one was related to her, and so they seized her and threw her into the water. In vain she tried to get hold of the edge of the raft; they cut her fingers off, and lo! as she sank to the bottom the stumps of her fingers became alive in the water and bobbed up round the raft like seals. That was how the seals came. But Nuliajuk herself sank to the bottom of the sea. There she became a spirit, the sea spirit, and she became the mother of the sea beasts, because the seals had formed out of her fingers that were cut off. And she also became mistress of everything else alive, the land beasts too, that mankind had to hunt.
>
> In that way she obtained great power over mankind, who had despised her and thrown her into the sea. She became the most feared of all spirits, the most powerful, and the one who more than any other controls the destinies of men. For that reason almost all taboo is directed against her, though only in the dark period while the sun is low, and it is cold and windy on earth; for then life is most dangerous to live. (Rasmussen, 1931, p. 225-227)

Nâlungiaq continues by sharing information about this goddess's realm and the beings that live there. This account is unusually detailed and discusses the angakkuq's relationship to the sea mother:

> Nuliajuk lives in a house on the bed of the sea. At the bottom of the sea there are lands just as on the earth above the sea, and Nuliajuk lives in a house that is arranged in the same manner as those that humans live in.
>
> In her house Nuliajuk lives remote from all, hasty in her anger and terrible in her might when she wishes to punish mankind. She notices every little breach of taboo, for she knows everything. Whenever people have been indifferent towards her by not observing taboo, she hides all the animals; the seals she shuts up in her in·aut: a drip-basin that she has under her lamp. As long as they are inside it, there are no animals to hunt in the sea, and mankind has to starve; the shamans then have to summon their helping spirits and conjure her to be kind again. Some shamans are content to let their helping spirits work for mankind, they themselves remaining in their houses summoning and conjuring in a trance, whereas others rush down to her themselves to fight her, to overcome her and appease her. But there are also some who draw Nuliajuk herself up to the surface of the land. They do it in this way: they make a hook fast to the end of a long seal thong and throw it out of the entrance passage; the spirits set the hook fast in her, and the shaman hauls her up into the passage. There everybody can hear her speaking. But the entrance from the passage into the living room must be closed with a block of snow, and this block, ukkuaq, Nuliajuk keeps on trying to break into pieces in order to get into the house to frighten everybody to death. And there is great fear in the house. But the shaman watches the ukkuaq, and so Nuliajuk never gets into the house. Only when she has promised the shaman to release all the seals into the sea again does he take her off the hook and allow her to go down into the depths again.

> In that way a shaman, who is only a human being, can subdue Nuliajuk and save people from hunger and misery by means of his words and his helping spirits.
>
> In their house Nuliajuk is surrounded by a lot of frightful beings. Just inside the entrance to her house passage sits kataum inua, the ruler of the passage, who keeps an exact record of all the breaches of taboo committed by mankind up on earth. Everything Ise sees and hears he passes on to Nuliajuk, and he tries in every possible way to scare the shamans who want to go in to her, so that they will abandon their intention of mollifying her.
>
> A long way in the passage itself there is a big black dog, and he too keeps watch to see that none but the greatest shamans, of whom he is afraid, get into the house.
>
> Nuliajuk herself lives with Isarrataitsoq: "the one with no wings or the one with no arms"—a woman, but nobody knows who she is. She has the same husband as Nuliajuk, and he is a little sea scorpion.
>
> A child, too, lives with Nuliajuk; she is called Ungâq: "the one who screams like a child"; it is a baby that was once stolen from a sleeping mother when her husband was out hunting at the breathing holes.
>
> This is all we know of Nuliajuk, the sea spirit, who gives seals to mankind, it is true, but who would much rather that mankind, from whom she once received no pity when she lived on earth, perished too. (Rassmussen, 1931, p. 225-227)

Much mystery surrounds this woman of the sea. According to stories, she lives in the darkness of the deep ocean. The means of her control and the limits of her power vary from region to region, however most of the Inuit groups that know her agree that she is a dangerous and powerful woman. From stories and personal accounts, it seems that this being is one to avoid. To draw her attention can be dangerous to individuals and their families. Dearth, hunger, sickness, and misfortune are the tools with which she punishes those who have offended her. And she is easily offended. The mother of the sea mammals is easy to anger, quick to punish, and difficult to pacify. Modern stories and accounts of this mysterious woman may paint her as a benevolent being, but stories of the past tell a different tale.

The Giants of the North

Years ago when the Arctic was still young, many giants lived and hunted on these northern lands. Some of these beings were so large that they could stride fjords and even wade into the ocean to catch whales with their bare hands. The animals hunted by these beings were enormous. Regular polar bears were often mistaken as lemmings or small foxes. The great giants hunted larger animals such as bowhead whales or nanurliut, the giant polar bear. The giants were few in numbers and warred amongst themselves. Inuit generally tried to avoid these colossal beings, however, at least one giant befriended Inuit and even adopted an Inuit man as his own son. These mighty beings are called *inukpasugjuit.*

Many accounts and descriptions of these great giants can be found throughout Inuit mythology. Atqãralq, a Caribou Inuit informant, shared some information about a giant. This quotation illustrates the size and power of the great giants:

> Our forefathers have told us about inukpäk, a giant, whom they saw in times long past. He was so tall that his hood reached up to heaven, and when he walked across the country, he could stride over even the greatest of rivers and wade through all the lakes, and even when he went out midway into the salt sea, the water only came up to his knees. Once inukpäk stole away a man who was out hunting. And so huge was inukpäk, and so small was the man, that he tucked him away in under the lace of his kamik.

> That is all we have heard tell of inukpäk. (Rasmussen, 1930, p. 108)

Another Inuit informant from Cumberland Sound shared a description of an inukpasugjuk. Again, from the description, the awesome size and strength of these beings can be imagined:

> It is said that a giant used to bail out of the sea with his hands the people and their boats. Then he put the people into a large box; and, as he watched it all the time, they were unable to escape. It is also said of him that he caught whales just as one would catch sculpins, by straddling a fiord and fishing in this manner. (Boas, 1901, p. 304-5)

These towering individuals were not the only giants in the north. Throughout Inuit mythology, from Greenland to the Bering Sea, many lesser giants can be found in traditional stories and in recorded interviews about personal encounters. These strange and powerful beings often ate people and some would hunt down children that strayed too far from their camps. According to George Kappianaq, an elder from Iglulik, these mighty beings were called *inugaruligasugjuit*. Inugaruligasugjuit are larger than humans, but smaller than the great giants of the north. (Kappianaq & Nutaraq, 2001, p. 99)

There have not been sightings of inukpasugjuit for some time. No one knows what happened to all of these magnificent beings. Perhaps they killed each other in great battles. Numerous references suggest that they were not kind to each other and often fought. A few informants suggested that many of the giants have turned into stone. Strange rock formations close to several communities are said to be the impression of giant feet or the result of a giant that had turned to stone.

A storyteller from the west coast of Hudson Bay supported

this conclusion and shared the following information with an explorer:

> At the time when the Eskimo reached this country, there were many giants here who caught fish by dipping them out of the water in their hands. These may be seen now, turned into stone, at Repulse Bay, where their footprints may also be seen. (Boas, 1907, p. 539)

Perhaps the reason for the absence of giants from the Arctic is even simpler. In 1930, Knud Rasmussen interviewed an Inuit informant close to Iglulik who suggested another possibility as to why we have not seen any giants for many years:

> There was once a giant so tall that it used to wade out into the sea and catch walrus with its hands. The giant was a mighty sleeper, and when it lay down on the ground and went to sleep, the plants of the earth grew up over it, and ordinary womenfolk would go gathering fuel without knowing they were walking over a live giant lying there asleep. (Rasmussen, 1930, p. 114)

If these beings rested without moving for so long that the grasses and lichen grew all over them, then perhaps they are still around us, sleeping under rocks and vegetation, hidden from all but the keenest eyes.

There are too many stories of giants in Inuit myths and legends to present them all. The remainder of this chapter showcases stories of giants from all over the Arctic. Many inukpasugjuit and inugaruligasugjuit are included in these stories.

Many Inuit groups tell a story of an enormous giant who adopted an Inuit man as his son. Marianne Pujuat Taparti, of Rankin Inlet, shared her version of the story of an inukpasugjuk that adopted a human son:

There was an inukpasugjuk who had adopted a human. It carried the human in a lace eyelet on its ankle (a loop outside the kamik located at the ankle used as an eyelet as it was not possible to make holes in the kamik). This was possible because an inukpasugjuk is a huge creature.

Why didn't this creature carry the baby human on its back? Or carry him in its hood? Instead, the giant decided to carry the child in an eyelet near the ankle.

So the child grew up with the inukpasugjuk.

The inukpasugjuk encounters another inukpasugjuk that is carrying two fish, but they are actually whales. The inukpasugjuk asks for one of the fish but the other inukpasugjuk did not want to give one up. The two inukpasugjuit begin to fight each other and the one with the human starts to lose, so he tells his child to cut the Achilles' tendon of the other inukpasugjuk. And that is a big tendon we have behind our foot. So the human child goes and cuts the Achilles' tendon. The inukpasugjuk with the fish is defeated with the help of the human. As the inukpasugjuk with the fish was getting beaten he was calling out to his wife. She heard his calls and was coming to defend her husband. The ground was even shaking from the bouncing of her humongous breast because she was an inukpasugjuk herself. That must have been scary.

The female inukpasugjuk and the inukpasugjuk with the adopted human start to fight. The inukpasugjuk tells the child to cut the Achilles' tendons again. Of course the small person beside the giants is trying to cut the tendons to help his parent. The child is said to have grown quite big too, because of being raised by an inukpasugjuk. Of course the two working together won again because they were outnumbering their opponent. Now the couple was slain.

For some reason the two that were victorious decided to follow the tracks of the slain female. Along her tracks, they found the child of the giant couple on the ground. The inukpasugjuk threatened to kill the big baby.

The baby told them he could kick and the land would cave in, so the inukpasugjuk told him to try. When the baby did kick, the inukpasugjuk and his son became very frightened. The inukpasugjuk and the human killed the baby out of fear.

And that is the story of the inukpasugjuk. (Marianne Pujuat Taparti, personal communication, 2005)

Manelaq, a Netsilik informant, shared a version of the story about the famous giant, Inugpasugssuk. This giant was a great friend to many Inuit. This version of the story introduces the reader to a nanurluk, the giant polar bear of the Arctic:

> There was once a giant named Inugpasugssuk. He was so big that his lice were as large as lemmings. He used to fish for salmon at Kitingijait, a wide and enormous ravine in the Netsilik land. Through the ravine runs a river that is so deep that no one can see the bottom. There Inugpasugssuk used to catch salmon, standing astride over the ravine. He took the salmon with his hands when they lay under the stones, and although they were very big fish he called them salmon fry.
>
> Sometimes he caught seals. He waded out into the sea with a stick in his hand and killed the seals when they bobbed up out of the water, striking them with his stick.
>
> Once he waded out at Arviligjuaq as usual to catch seals.
>
> He was always very careful with humans and always afraid of doing them harm, and therefore he used to move those that lived on the low, flat shores up on to the higher islands in the bay. For it happened once that he had to swim a stroke in order to get at a seal, and it had made a wave so enormous that it washed people out into the fjord. That wave went far in over all the land in the vicinity and washed quantities of fish up on to the shore, it is those we now find as fossils and use as wick trimmers for our lamps. There are all kinds of small fish: kanajrqât: small sea scorpions; ijitot: small cod with large eyes; kiiuit: sticklebacks; aqalugkht: salmon fry; ogagluit: cod; and many other kinds.
>
> Another time Inugpasugssuk raised a wave that also flooded the whole district of Arviligjuaq. As usual he was out sealing and accidentally struck his own penis; it shot up out of the water but was so far away that he thought it was

a seal putting its head up. The pain made him tumble over backwards so that he sat down, and that movement raised a sea that went right in over the land.

Inugpasugssuk was very fond of humans and often camped close to where they were. He once fell in love with an Inuk woman and exchanged wives with her husband. The exchange turned out so badly, however, that Inugpasugssuk never tried it again. The Inuk man, who was lying with Inugpasugssuk's wife, fell into her genitals and never came up again. He dissolved in her inside and his bones came out with her urine. But the Inuk woman, with whom lnugpasugssuk was lying, was split right across and died.

Inugpasugssuk was sorry he had killed a human. To console himself he took a tiguaq, a foster son, from among the humans, and he reared him in such a manner that he grew and grew and became much bigger than humans usually grow. The foster son helped the giant with all kinds of work, and, when evening came, and the giant lay down to sleep, he loved to be loused; but his foster son, who was afraid to take the big lice with his naked hands, always had mittens on when he loused him.

One evening, it is said, the giant gave his foster son two stones, a small one and a big one, and spoke to him thus:

"Tonight I expect that big game will come to our house. If a bear should appear in the ravine you must waken me, and you must do it by first knocking my head with the little stone. If I do not wake up, take the big stone and thump my head with it."

Then the giant lay down to sleep and the foster son kept a look out through the window.

It was not long before a big bear appeared away up the ravine, and at once the son knocked his foster father on the

head with the small stone. The giant woke up, saw the bear, and laughed heartily, saying:

"Yes, but that's only a fox."

Nevertheless he went out and killed it, and lay down to sleep again. The boy kept watch again, and it was not long before another animal appeared, and this time it was so big that in the ravine it turned quite dark. Once more the foster son took the small stone and hit the giant's head with it. But by this time the giant had become sleepy and, as he did not wake up quickly enough, the boy seized the big stone and began to hammer away at his temples with it. Only then did he awake. Looking up towards the ravine a slight shiver passed through his great body; it was hunting ardour, and he said:

"Yes, this time it is a real bear," and, taking his foster son and placing him in his putuaq: the strap round his kamik, ran out and killed the bear.

Once Inugpasugssuk's foster son wanted to visit his family, but as they lived far away, and he did not know the way, the giant gave him his magic wand, saying: "Every evening, when you lie down to sleep, you must stick this wand into the ground. When you wake up the wand will always have fallen over and will be pointing in the direction you have to go."

And it happened as the giant had said, and the foster son safely reached his old village. But it is told that he had now grown so tall that he could no longer get into the houses of humans. So he soon went back to the giant, and since then nothing has been heard of them. (Rassmussen, 1931, p. 252-254)

In 1901, Franz Boas published "Eskimo of Baffin Land and Hudson Bay" in the *Bulletin of the American Museum of Natural*

History. In that volume he recorded many stories from Inuit on Baffin Island and the communities surrounding Hudson Bay. The following stories about giants come directly from his interviews with Inuit informants around Cumberland Sound (east coast of Baffin Island).

The first story from Cumberland Sound is about Koodlowetto, the giant. Although Koodlowetto is described as "a man of monstrous size" he must have been an inugaruligasugjuk (lesser giant), judging by the fact that he needed to brace himself when he harpooned a walrus. A true giant probably would not even have recognized a walrus for what it was; instead it might have thought it was a large lemming or fat siksik:

> At Anganichen, beyond Aggo, lived a man of monstrous size, whose name was Koodlowetto. His sister was as large as he. One day he went hunting, and came to a place where a number of walrus had made a hole through the ice. He got ready to harpoon them, and as soon as one appeared, he harpooned it. Then he took hold of his line, and got in position to hold the walrus when it should dive. While he was standing there, he stumbled on a small piece of ice which was probably thrown out by the walrus when they made the hole. He fell down, and, as the end of his line was fastened round his left wrist, he was dragged into the water. He was so large, however, that he was able to take hold of the ice at one side of the hole with one hand, while he held on to the opposite side with the other. Thus he held on until the line eased up. Then he was able to crawl out of the hole, haul in the walrus, and kill it. When he reached home, he told the people what had happened. Another day he went off with the other people to seal. In the evening a man by the name of Ikalakjew passed him on his way home. He invited him to sit down on his sledge; but as soon as he sat down, the sledge broke to pieces, and both had to walk home. (Boas, 1901, p. 195-6)

The next Cumberland Sound story presented here is about a female inukpasugjuk. Female inukpasugjuit seem to be less common than males. However, female inugaruligasugjuit seem to be more common than male inugaruligasugjuit. As you can see with Inupassaqdjung, she mistakes whales for catfish ("catfish" is perhaps a mistaken translation for sculpin which are common in the Arctic waters). Mistaking huge animals for smaller species seems to be a characteristic of the great giants:

> In Saumia lived a female monster, Inupassaqdjung, as tall as the island Kikertaqdjuaq. She used to straddle one of the fjords to look for catfish, as she said; but she really meant to catch whales. Whenever she saw one, she lifted it up in the hollow of her hand, and conveyed it to her mouth. One day some Eskimo had caught a whale, and while they were trying to kill it, the giantess came along and lifted them all up—boats, whale, and people. The whale was striking about with its tail, which amused her, and she cried, "Lil, lil, lil!" When it was dead, she landed whale, boat, and men the shore.
>
> In the winter she asked a man to become her husband. She said to him, "Place a stone beside me, and if you see a bear, take the stone in your hands, and strike my head with it until I wake up." After she had been asleep a short time, the man saw a bear coming. He took a stone, struck her head with it until she awoke, and showed her the bear that was approaching on the ice. She cried, "That is not a bear, it a little fox." When it came nearer, she took it up. It was a bear, although she called it a fox. She said to her husband, "Do you see those bunches of seaweed? When you see the spaces between them filled, that you may call a bear." What she called seaweed were two islands with an enormous space between them. She went to sleep again. After a while he saw something coming which filled the space between the islands. He took a stone and struck the head of the giantess until she awoke. He shouted, "There

is a large bear yonder!" She jumped up, saw the bear, and said, "Indeed this is a bear!" Before she went in pursuit, however, she put her husband inside the loop at the side of her boot, which is used for tightening the shoestrings. She took a stone and killed the enormous bear with it. Then she took it ashore, flensed it, and put the meat away. They had no house, but they lived on the land, the sky being their roof. (Boas, 1901, p. 196-7)

The next Cumberland Sound story is about an inugaruligasugjuk named Nareya. Nareya is a grave-robber and a glutton. His huge appetite is his undoing and ultimately brings fog into the world of the Inuit:

> Nareya was a huge man, who lived in the interior of the country. When running down caribou, he wound his body with thongs to prevent him from running too fast, and to steady his belly, which was of enormous size. He overtook the caribou easily, and knocked them down with stones. He would eat the meat of three caribou at one meal, then he would go to the river, where he had a place scooped out large enough for his belly, lie down, and drink of the water until he had enough. He used to lie there until he felt hungry again.
>
> One day a man who was out caribou-hunting came to the place at the side of the river where Nareya was lying. The man watched him for a long time, until finally Nareya looked up and saw him. He arose at once, and ran after the man, who tried to escape; but Nareya overtook him and killed him. When the hunter did not return to the village, his friends became very anxious, and one of them went in search of him. He did not find him; but on his return, he discovered that the bodies of the dead had been taken away from the graves. Finally he came to the place where Nareya was lying, at the side of the water.
>
> Then he went home and told what he had seen. The people did not know what to do. One of them offered to pretend to be dead and to have himself buried under stones. He expected that he would be taken away like the bodies of the dead, and that he would thus discover the robber. The people carried him out of the house, and covered him up with stones. When it was nearly morning, Nareya discovered the new grave. He took the stones off, fastened a thong around the body in two places, put it on his back, and carried it away. When he came to his home, he took off the rope and put the body down.

The man, who was an angakok, pretended to be dead; but when he thought nobody was looking, he blinked with his eyes, and saw Nareya, his wife, and his child, in the tent. Now the man knew that this was the monster that had been taking away the bodies of his friends, and he thought that he must also have killed the caribou-hunter. He heard Nareya tell how he had eaten three caribou, and even more, in a single day. Nareya told his wife to make a fire and to cook the body which he had brought, meaning the man who had pretended to be dead. While the woman was starting the fire, the child thought he noticed the eyes of the man moving. He said so; but Nareya replied, "Never mind. Yesterday, when I brought the body here, it seemed to be very heavy." Now he turned to his wife and asked, "Is the water hot?" When she answered in the affirmative, the man jumped up and knocked Nareya down. Then he ran away as fast as he could.

Soon Nareya recovered, and pursued him. The man, by means of sorcery, made various things to allure his pursuer and to distract his attention. Nareya stopped for a time, but soon continued his pursuit. When he had nearly reached the fugitive, the latter, by means of sorcery, made a great many berries. When Nareya saw them, he stopped, and picked and ate a great many. Meanwhile the man had run over a hill. When he reached the foot of the hill, and saw the monster gaining upon him, he made a river. Nareya reached the river, and, on seeing the man on the other side, he asked him, "How did you cross?" The man replied, "I drank all the water until I was able to wade through the river." Then Nareya lay down and began to drink. He almost emptied the river, went across, and when he came to the other side, shook the water out of his sleeves. His stomach was so full of water that it made him burst, and he died. A mist arose from him, and from it all the mist and fog originated. The man lost his way in the fog, but after some time it cleared away, and he reached home safely. (Boas, 1901, p. 176-178)

All Inuit groups seem to have stories about giant beings. Hinrich Rink collected many myths and legends from Inuit and published them in *Tales and Traditions of the Eskimo* in 1875. The following stories are from this collection.

The first two stories come from Labrador. These two stories seem to describe lesser giants. The first story shows the adversarial relationship some of these lesser giants had with the neighbouring Inuit:

> Sikuliarsiujuitsok, on account of his great size, was unable to walk upon new ice. He, all by himself, caught a whale from his kayak. But he was much dreaded and hated, and never ventured to sleep in strange places. He was, however, once persuaded to stay for a night in a snow hut; and being too big to find room in it, he lay all doubled up, and allowed his feet to be tied together. In this condition he was hauled out and killed, but not before he himself had killed four men in the struggle. He had three sisters, one of whom had three sons, likewise powerful men. They had an enclosure, fenced in with stones, into which they enticed all those they intended to kill. (Rink, 1875, p. 449)

The second story is about a very powerful man, whose feats of strength prevented him from losing his wife:

> A man named Aklaujak was of immense strength. Once, when away on a reindeer-hunt, his brothers robbed him of his wife. But the mother, who from a high hill observed him sitting in his kayak and seizing two large reindeers by the antlers and drowning them by holding them under water, hastened down and persuaded the wife to return to him, on which the brothers took flight. (Rink, 1875, p. 449)

This next story, collected by Rink, comes from Greenland. It shows the weakness of giants—their feet and Achilles tendons.

Cutting the tendons in the heel is often the preferred method of falling a giant:

> The people from the south (or east) and those from the north (or west) were at war with each other. The latter had a powerful champion, who was sitting on the top of Kangersuak to watch the Southlanders passing by. A man who had been killed by him left a son, who practised angakok science, and revenged his father by inducing the giant to walk with him over a marshy plain, where he went down, and from beneath pierced the feet of the giant, and afterwards killed him. (Rink, 1875, p. 449-450)

This next story describes an adventure of an orphan named Inoosarsuk. Orphans are common characters in Inuit stories. Their mistreatment usually ends with the orphan taking revenge on the abuser. In this story, Inoosarsuk meets up with a huge kayaker. This type of giant is called a *kayarissat*. Rink describes the kayarissat as "kayakmen of extraordinary size" who used single-bladed paddles (p. 47). These massive beings were always met while hunting in the ocean, far away from land. These beings were said to be skilled in sorcery and could raise storms and bring bad weather if it served their purpose:

> The orphan boy Inoosarsuk was greatly loved by his foster-mother, but not by his foster-father. One day, when the father was out on a seal-hunt, the mother told Inoosarsuk she was tired of seal-flesh, and ordered him out in her husband's other kayak to catch some frog-fish. He remonstrated, saying that his father had forbidden him to take the kayak; but still she went on desiring him to go, at the same time assuring him she would clean and put it back all right in its place.

Notwithstanding, the father coming home observed that it had been used, and beat Inoosarsuk till he could not move for pain. Another day his mother went on persuading him in the same way to take the kayak in order to go out and get her some quannek (the eatable stalk of Angelica archangelica), growing near the shore, a little up the firth. But when he had ascended the hills in order to fetch her some, and came back to the beach, he found, to his great alarm, that the tide had carried away the half-jacket belonging to his foster-father's kayak.

On approaching home he got so frightened at the thought of his foster-father that he passed it by and turned right out to sea. Having rowed beyond the outermost islands he suddenly remembered his two amulets, a quannek and an old whetstone; and jumping out on a flake of drift-ice, he planted one of his newly-gathered stalks, calling out, "Thus shalt thou remain standing erect,"—an invocation to secure him calm weather.

Like Giviok, he passed by the ocean-lice for Akilinek, and having first encountered the cannibals, he afterwards fell in with the women who captured fishes by putting bladders to them at low tide. From the cannibals' chimney a black smoke arose in the air, but from that of the latter a white smoke was seen.

Among these he was very kindly treated, but still he at last grew tired of his sojourn; and one day pretending to row a little in the neighbourhood, he took himself far off and fled to the south. At length he arrived at a wild firth; but thinking it too long to enter, he resolved merely to cross the inlet to the opposite shore.

When half-way across he saw what he fancied was a rock; but on coming closer he found it to be an enormously big kayaker, who took hold of him and lifted him up quite easily, kayak and all, in one hand, and put him down before

> himself on his own vessel, intending to take him home as an amulet for his little daughter. When they approached the homestead of the giant, something like a big iceberg was standing in front of the house; on closer inspection it proved to be an enormous gull, which the giant's daughter was in the act of catching.
>
> Inoosarsuk was now brought up to the house and put upon a shelf near the window. During the night he took a fancy to some very nice-looking eatables lying behind the lamp. He managed to slide down on the side ledge, but finding it quite filled up by the giant's sleeping daughter, without any room left where to put down his foot, he had no choice left but to step along her one leg; unfortunately he lost his footing and fell down.
>
> The giant's daughter on being awakened in this way, and unconsciously grasping him, had nearly eaten him up, but luckily remembered that he was her little amulet. The giant seeing Inoosarsuk's dismay and utter dejection, at length put him down on the floor, and covered him up with his large cloak, saying, "Thou shalt grow as big as that, as big as that." He forthwith commenced to grow, and was soon as tall as the daughter, after which the giant furnished him with a kayak of suitable size. He now remembered his foster-parents; and longing to take revenge for the many blows he had formerly got, he crossed the ocean, and soon found the place where they had formerly lived. But the house was laid waste, and the old people buried beneath its ruins. He then returned to pass the rest of his days at Akilinek. (Rink, 1875, p. 428-430)

The following account of a giant comes from an Inuit woman from northern Greenland named Anarfwik. In this story, the giant is so large that he wants to use a kayak as an amulet. However, there are Inuit in the kayaks and they do not want to spend the rest of their lives trapped in a giant's amulet:

There was once a giant; he was so big that he called the polar bear a fox.

One day he saw five kayaks and thought he would like to use the men as amulets; and so he scooped them up in his hand, brought them home to his house, and put them on a shelf under the lamp.

Then the giant ate polar bear and whale-beef and fell asleep.

He was so big that his lice were foxes.

And when a few foxes had slipped in and begun to bite his head, he muttered—

"Don't drip the lamp-black over me!"

He thought that it was the men, pouring lamp-black down. They positively shook with fear.

Then they tried to get down, lowering themselves by seal-skin thongs.

And then all at once the giant began to talk in his sleep.

"Tread on the lamp-stone!" he muttered. The men shuddered.

At last they reached the floor, and ran towards the door; but the threshold was so high that they very nearly failed to get over it.

At last they were free, and ran down to their kayaks and escaped.

When the giant awoke and discovered that the men had escaped, he cried, annoyed with himself—

> "Oh, why did I not tear the eyes out of their heads!" (Rasmussen, 1908, p.178-9)

The mistreatment of an orphan is a common theme in Inuit stories. In this next story, from northern Greenland, an informant named Qilerneq tells of an ill-treated orphan fortunate enough to meet up with a giant. This giant takes pity on the small orphan and helps him find the power to exact revenge on the people who have abused him:

> Once upon a time there was a little orphan boy whose name was Kâvssagssuk. He slept in the passage, among the dogs, and warmed himself on the roof, by the air-hole through which the warm air streamed out. When the dogs in the passage were beaten, they would strike Kâvssagssuk too. They gave him no other food than walrus skin, which he could not chew, because they amused themselves by pulling his teeth out.
>
> A man of the name of Umerdlugtôrssuaq (the "Great Broad-nosed One") used to have great fun with him, and would lift him up by his nostrils, and shake him well; this made his nostrils bigger and bigger.
>
> He had two grandmothers: the one, his father's mother, beat him whenever she saw him; but the other, his mother's mother, dried his foot-wear; for she was sorry for him, because he was the child of her daughter, who was a woman like herself.
>
> When the light came, and the nights were dark no longer, Kâvssagssuk went off on a journey on foot; and he met a big man, who stood on the beach by the tide belt, flensing. And he began to shout for meat; but it only rang in the ears of the giant. At last the giant heard what the boy said.

"Here, I will give you meat," said the giant, and threw it to him without looking at him; the orphan could hardly drag it away, it was so much, and so he made himself a meat-pit.

The day after, he wanted to go and look at his meat-pit, and when he could not find it, he burst out crying. The giant caught sight of the little fellow standing there crying, and said:

"Well, is it the meat? I thought it belonged to someone else; it was I who took it. But shall we not go for a little walk together?" He was so anxious to console the little fellow. And so they went.

Then the giant started to run and pushed a large stone on the one side, so that it began to spin round and round. "And now you," said he, to amuse Kâvssagssuk, and he ran up and tried to push the stone, but only fell down. "Try again, and then again!" but the little one found it quite impossible to do it. "And now again, go on trying," and at last he really managed to make the stone spin round. Then they tried bigger stones, and at last Kâvssagssuk could make great rocks spin round.

"Now go home," said the giant to him; "I will send you meat; three bears shall come to your village in the winter." And so Kâvssagssuk went home. Down by the houses he went up to the umiaq [boat] of his tormentor, which was frozen fast in the ice. He tore it up with one wrench, and then he went inside and lay down amongst the dogs.

The next day the Broad-nosed One was uneasy when he saw that the umiaq had been torn up. "I wonder who can have done that?" he said; "we must have a giant amongst us; perhaps it is you there," said he, and he pointed to Kâvssagssuk, to make fun of him.

One day later in the winter, as Kâvssagssuk was sitting barefooted inside, having his kamiks dried, there was a shout that three bears were in sight; none of the dogs dared attack them, because they were so big and strong.

His tormentor shouted in through the windows to him to mock him.

"Oh! if I only had a weapon; lend me a pair of short indoor kamiks!" said the orphan, and his cousin Sorqardluk lent them to him.

Then he sprang out, down to the edge of the ice, and the hard snow flew up round him as he ran.

"Only look at Kâvssagssuk," called out the people; "he is mad, he has gone mad." Then he ran up to the bears. First he seized the mother, and wrung her neck; he then seized her grown-up cubs by the throats, and dashed their heads together, that they grew rigid. The mother he flung over his shoulder and the cubs he took under his arms. They seemed to weigh nothing, and in this way he carried them up.

But his old tormentor was very busy, and now he fled with his two wives.

Then Kâvssagssuk made himself a very large pot, and piled up firewood and made a fire. He put huge pieces of bear's flesh in the pot. But the old grandmother who used to beat him he seized and threw into the fire. She was burnt right up; the only thing that was left of her was her stomach.

The other grandmother was about to run away too, but her he held back, saying, "You always dried my kamiks!"

Kâvssagssuk then wanted to pursue his tormentor, and his cousin went with him.

The Broad-nosed One had stopped in his flight off a steep cliff, where he had set up his tent. There they took turns to keep watch, for they expected the pursuers. But at last they had all fallen asleep.

When Kâvssagssuk came near to their tent they were all lying asleep. So he seized hold of his old tormentor by his nostrils, and carried him out to the edge of the cliff, and gave him a good shaking over the precipice. When he put him down on the ground again, both nostrils were split, and he could do nothing but hold his hands to his face, but Kâvssagssuk went and knocked over the tent, saying—

"Umerdlugtôrssuaq, now I shall take your wives!" and so he carried them off, but his old tormentor died of the wounds in his nose.

When he got back, Kâvssagssuk revenged himself on all those who had ill-treated him before, and then he went away to the people who live in the south.

It is told that down there he made himself a kayak, and went out fishing with the men, but his tremendous strength brought with it a strong desire to terrify people, and when he began to squeeze children's bodies till their intestines came out, his fellow fishermen harpooned him one day, on a kayak expedition, and killed him.

That is what we have heard tell. (Rasmussen, 1908, p. 201-4)

Like most Inuit groups, the Inuit of Labrador have many stories of Inuit beings. This next story depicts a giant who uses his size to terrorize his neighbours. This bold giant is bested by an unlikely opponent:

A long time ago there lived in Saglek Bay a giant who played the tyrant over the people there. He would do no work, but stole seals from the hunters. They did not dare to show their resentment because he was so big and strong. Finally they killed him by getting him to allow himself to be bound.

In the same village there lived a dwarf named Alasuq. He lived alone with his mother. His father had died when he was young, and he had supported his mother ever since, like a man. Although he was so small, he was very strong. He was a jolly little fellow and well liked by all the people.

One day the giant, who was always boasting what he could do and frightening the hunters, challenged them to a kayak race around an island in the bay. None of them dared to accept, but little Alasuq said he would try him. Everyone laughed at him, but it did not turn him from his purpose.

He laid aside his usual paddle, and made himself an enormously large one, larger even than the giant's. It had holes in the middle for hand grips.

When he came out to race, all the people remarked about it, particularly the giant, who made fun of the little man and his big paddle.

But when they started, no one laughed anymore. The little fellow handled his paddle so strongly that he would have broken an ordinary paddle. He quickly outdistanced the giant. When he was rounding the island, long before he came in sight, the people could hear his kayak, shish, cleaving the water. The giant was badly beaten, but took it goodnaturedly, as, of course, he had to, having challenged the hunters.

The little dwarf lived for a long time afterwards, and was always much respected by the people. (Hawkes, 1961, p. 150-151)

During a Canadian expedition to the Arctic from 1913-18, Diamond Jenness recorded many Inuit myths and legends. This next story, told by a Copper Inuit informant named Hiqilag, describes a female giant named Nahaingaiaq. Nahaingaiaq is a cannibal who eventually makes the mistake of trying to hunt down an Inuit hunter armed with a bow and arrows:

> There once lived a giant woman named Nahaingaiaq, the daughter of a man named Akuiugyuk. She carried an adze and an ulo for killing people, whom she used to slip inside her coat and carry off. Once she found an Eskimo fishing on a lake. He fled, but she pursued him and was on the point of seizing him when he turned and shot her with his bow and arrow. He left her lying where she fell, but other Eskimos found the body and laid it out properly in burial. (Jenness, 1926, p. 83)

This next story was told by Anauyuk, a Dolphin and Union Strait angakkuq. Here we see that an Inuit group was not helpless against a giant. Through the power of chanting magical verses, an angakkuq was able to change the giant into stone:

> Long ago a giant crossed over from the mainland to the most southern of the Liston and Sutton islands, in Dolphin and Union strait. It was midsummer, and the sea was free of ice, but so tall was he that the water hardly reached above his knees. The sun did not see him as he crossed. As soon as he reached the island he took up two huge boulders and began to toss them up in the air, juggling with them. There was a party of Eskimos living on Putulik, the most northern island of the group, and they were terrified at his appearance. One of their shamans chanted a spell against him, and the giant immediately dropped his stones and tried to flee, but before he reached the edge of the island he was changed to rock. Now only his nose and eyebrows are visible; formerly he wore a red belt, but the

> wind has carried that away. His juggling stones can still be seen lying where he dropped them, on top of the rock Ahungahungaq. (Jenness, 1926, p. 84)

A story recorded from Inuit living in the Cumberland Sound region describes a giant couple that helped feed Inuit who were starving. These giants stayed with the Inuit group for some time, helping them find caribou for food and clothing:

> At Qeqertaunang, near Kinertun in Aggo, there lived a man whose name was Alainang. He had a wife as large as himself. Her name was Eyeeyvolwalow. His bow was very large, and his arrows were so strong that they could be used to support the drying-frame for clothing. They were broad and as long as a person is tall. One winter he crossed from Davis Strait through Pangnirtung to Cumberland Sound, and travelled along the coast to Aukarneling. From there he started across land to the head of Frobisher Bay. He carried for travelling-provisions a bag made of the whole skin of a ground-seal, which was filled half with meat and half with blubber. Besides, he had on his sledges meat and blubber for his dogs and for his lamp. When he reached Frobisher Strait, he found the people starving, and he gave them food to eat. His wife was so large that she required two whole caribou skins for her boots. The giant staid [stayed] there for some time, hunting caribou; and on one of his hunting trips he remained away from the village for one whole month. The people said to his wife, "Your husband is staying away long. What may have become of him?" She replied, "He has not lost his way; he is looking for food. He will return before the new moon. He always does so when he goes caribou-hunting." At the end of the month he returned, and brought a little caribou meat. Then he told the people that he had found a great many caribou, and that he had tried to drive them towards the village, but that he had been unable to do so. On the following day he asked a man to accompany him, and they went together to

> the place where the caribou were. A great many that had been killed by the giant were still there, while others were still feeding. They were so tame that they allowed the men to touch them with their lances, and would not move: so they had to kill them right there. Then the people went out with their sledges to bring in the caribou-skins and caribou meat. The giant and his wife went back home, paddling along the coast. (Boas, 1907, p. 520-1)

When angered, an inukpasugjuk is a deadly enemy. On the west coast of Hudson Bay, an Inuit informant shared the following story that clearly demonstrates the power of an inukpasugjuk:

> Inuipassaksaq and his wife were out hunting. Their infant child was left at home. Then the Erqilit and Tornit came and killed the boy. When the Eskimo saw this, they told the giant what had happened. He became very angry, and asked the Eskimo to keep at a distance. Then he scooped up the waters of the sea—with all the whales, seals, and walruses that he happened to take up—and poured them over the land, so that his enemies were destroyed. The bones of these animals may be seen at the present day about five days' journey west from Repulse Bay. (Boas, 1907, p. 539)

This next story has several similarities to some of the preceding stories. One interesting difference is that an Inuit man was able to use magic to grow to the size of the inukpasugjuk he was about to fight. As has been seen in several previous stories, a human with a knife is often able to influence the outcome when two inukpasugjuit are fighting. This story was told by an Inuit informant from the west coast of Hudson Bay:

> A long time ago there was a man by the name of Inupajukjuk. He was so large that he could scoop up a walrus in the hollow of his hand. He used to speak of whales as of

> codfish. One day he walked out into the water and caught two whales, one in each hand. Two people watched him. After he had caught the whales, they asked him for some of the meat. Inupajukjuk had teeth like a squirrel, and the men said in asking him, "You have teeth like a squirrel." This made the giant angry, and he rushed to attack the men, but one of them turned himself into a giant of equal size. They wrestled, and endeavored to throw each other down. The other man had remained small, and he cut the sinews in the heel of Inupajukjuk. The latter fell and was stabbed to death, but before dying he called his wife to come and help him. She came at once, and seized the man who had transformed himself into a giant. She hit him on the head, and it seemed as though she were going to kill him, when the other man cut the sinews in her heel, and she fell and was killed. Then the two men started to go to the house of Inupajukjuk. On the way they found the young child of the latter, which his wife had dropped when she went to help her husband. It was lying on the ground, crying. The man who had remained small tried to raise the baby's head, but it was so large that he could not lift it. Then they went up to the house, and, on looking into the doorway, they saw two large boys sitting on the bed. They became frightened, because they thought they would not be able to vanquish the two boys, so they ran away. (Boas, 1901, p. 314)

Even though these northern giants have not been seen in many years, they still have a presence in traditional stories. Their reputed size and power has captured the imagination of Inuit storytellers across the Arctic. Numerous stories depict these giants as malevolent and destructive beings, though sometimes stories are told of giants who had good intentions and acted kindly towards Inuit. However, most giants, whether wicked or kind, are described as short tempered and dangerous when aroused. According to stories, the Arctic landscape has not felt the rumble of giant footsteps for many years. Some storytellers have suggested that these impressive beings have been sleeping for centuries hidden by the vegetation growing over them. So, perhaps one day we will feel the land shake again with the footsteps of these colossal monsters.

References

Boas, Franz (1888). Central Eskimo. *Bureau of American Ethnology, Annual Report 6*, 399-669.

Boas, Franz (1901). Eskimo of Baffin Land and Hudson Bay. *Bulletin of the American Museum of Natural History*, 15(1), 1-370.

Boas, Franz (1907). Second Report on the Eskimo of Baffin Land and Hudson Bay. *Bulletin of the American Museum of Natural History*, 15(2), 371-570

Hawkes, E.W. (1916). The Labrador Eskimo. *Canadian Department of Mines, Geological Survey, Memoir 91, no. 14, Anthropological Series*. Government Printing Bureau: Ottawa.

Jenness, D. (1926). Eskimo Folk-Lore. *Report of the Canadian Arctic Expedition 1913-18*, 13, F.A. Acland: Ottawa.

Kappianaq, G. & Nutaraq, C. (2001). *Inuit Perspectives on the 20th Century: Volume 2 - Travelling and Surviving on Our Land*. Nunavut Arctic College: Iqaluit.

Rasmussen, Knud (1908). *People of the Polar North*. Kegan Paul, Trench, Trübner & Co.: London.

Rasmussen, Knud (1929). *Intellectual Culture of the Iglulik Eskimo*. Gyldendalske Boghandel, Nordisk Forlag: Copenhagen.

Rasmussen, Knud (1930). *Observations on the Intellectual Culture of the Caribou Eskimo*. Gyldendalske Boghandel, Nordisk Forlag: Copenhagen.

Rasmussen, Knud (1931). *The Netsilik Eskimos: Social Life and Spiritual Culture*. Gyldendalske Boghandel, Nordisk Forlag: Copenhagen.

Rink, Hinrich (1875). *Tales and Traditions of the Eskimo*. William Blackwood and Sons: London.

About the Author

Neil Christopher moved to Resolute Bay, Nunavut, after teachers' college. He quickly fell in love with the North and has made it his home for over thirteen years. It was during his first few years in the North that Neil was introduced to the rich mythology of the Canadian Inuit. For the last eight years, Neil has been researching Inuit myths and legends and has subsequently published books on the topic for children, youth, and adults.

About the Illustrator

Mike Austin is an illustrator and tattoo artist with more than twenty-five years of experience. Mike was first introduced to the Inuit mythological pantheon through the work of Farley Mowat, and he has been transfixed by Northern mythology ever since. Mike strives to tell visual stories with his illustrations—both on paper and skin. His images have appeared in multiple books about Inuit mythology and he has represented Canada at several international tattoo competitions. Mike lives and works in London, Ontario.